THE ELEPHANT
IN THE DARK

by

IDRIES SHAH

The Octagon Press
London

SBN: 90086036 7

BP172
S46

Printed and bound in Great Britain by
Tonbridge Printers Ltd., Tonbridge, Kent.

THE ELEPHANT IN THE DARK
Christianity, Islam and the Sufis

GENEVA UNIVERSITY
LECTURES
1972/3

Christian scholars often say that Sufi theories are close to those of Christianity. Many Moslems maintain that they are essentially derived from Islam. The resemblance of many Sufi ideas to those of several religious and esoteric systems are sometimes taken as evidence of derivation. The Islamic interpretation is that religion is of one origin, differences being due to local or historical causes.

> Rumi, the Sufi teacher of 700 years ago, has emphasised and strikingly illustrated the last contention in his tale of the men who sought to examine an elephant by the sense of touch alone. Each thought that one part was the whole, and experienced it, moreover, in a manner slightly different from reality. The elephant was only, for one, a fan (an ear), for another a rope (the tail), for a third a pillar (a leg) and so on.

These lectures provide material for the consideration of common factors, in theory and in development, from the viewpoint of the idea of surrender to the Divine Will, reviewing some aspects of the interplay between Christians and Moslems, and introducing material from and about Sufis.

Grateful thanks are offered to the University of Geneva, to Dean Gabriel Widmer, to Professor N. Nissiotis and Dr. S. J. Samartha (Geneva), Professor Peter Antes (Feiburg University), Dr. B. Mukerji (Banaras University) and all the other participants in the work of the Ecumenical Institute at Bossey during my time there, for their generous spirit of service to scholarship and their help to me.

Idries Shah

CONTENTS

I

II

SALVATION AS A TOTAL SURRENDER TO GOD

I

I

The purpose of ecumenical studies, as it is at present employed, is to examine and encourage bases of religion, and the co-operation between people of various religions. Some Western dictionaries, I notice, define this activity as being concerned with the Christian church only; and the use of the word as confined solely to the Roman Catholic Church is noted in such authorities as the Oxford English Dictionary. 'Ecumenical', of course, is of Greek derivation, meaning *belonging to the whole world*. I shall assume, consistently with my presence here, that the narrower definitions just referred to are are not sustained by my audience. It is interesting to me, however, to note them: for they both indicate the assumption in some minds at least that a given way of thinking expressed in certain institutions is universal (on the negative side); and that my audience, at least, is contemporary enough in its objectivity to hear—at least—the ideas of those who do not belong to the theological formulations which constitute the background of their own attitudes—on the positive side. I need not say which one I prefer. Since I have been asked to contribute on 'Salvation as a Total Surrender to God: An Attempt at Dialogue Between Christians and Moslems', and Geneva University has honoured me by naming me a Visiting Professor and suggesting this subject, I would like, after expressing my gratitude for the opportunity to teach at this ancient and illustrious institution, to indicate that I propose to introduce the subject

(1) From an Islamic viewpoint;

(2) In its historical context, however rapidly;

(3) As something which has existed since the beginnings of Islam, nearly fifteen centuries ago, again with examples;

(4) As an opportunity of 'bridge-building' for the present and future, as well as the utilisation of the 'bridges' which are of considerable antiquity and tested strength.

Christian writers and scholars frequently complain that Moslems have distorted ideas about what the Christians believe, and what they practise. This may well be so, though as one who was brought up in an ancient and formal Moslem family with extensive experience of discussion with Moslems of many countries and every walk of life, I cannot recall anything analogous, even, to the report published not long ago by an American who attended a school run by the Arabian-American Oil Company in New York.*

'The questions "What is Islam?" and "Who was the Prophet Mohammed?"', he tells us, 'brought forth some interesting answers. One of our members thought that Islam was "a game of chance, similar to bridge".

*Butler, G. C., *Kings and Camels*, New York, 1960 pp. 16f.

Another said that it was "a mysterious sect founded in the South by the Ku Klux Klan." One gentleman believed it to be "an organization of American Masons who dress in strange costumes." The Prophet Mohammed was thought to be the man who "wrote the *Arabian Nights*". Another said that he was "an American Negro minister who was in competition with Father Divine in New York City." One of the more reasonable answers came from one of our men who said, "Mohammed had something to do with a mountain. He either went to the mountain, or it came to him." '

In quoting this extract, Professor James Kritzeck, the illustrious Orientalist (who is Director of the Institute for Advanced Religious Studies and Professor of Oriental Languages and History at Notre Dame University) comments: 'Even supposing these answers to be no more than facetious guesses, they still reveal an appalling ignorance on the part of American adults of better than average educational backgrounds—who were, moreover, on their way to employment in Saudi Arabia.'*

During the months in which I have been actively working on and thinking about the preparation of this material, I mentioned my task and the pleasure which I was taking in the prospect of contributing on this subject to a certain bishop. His words in comment were: 'Islam? That load of old rubbish? You don't mean to tell me that anyone in his right mind is taking any interest in it? Well, I suppose that we must take it as part and parcel of the present-day decay of standards and the resort of the foolish young to Oriental religions, and tomfoolery like astrology and witchcraft. Your friends would be better advised to seek solid Christian

*Anthology of Islamic Literature, London, 1964, (Introduction) pp. 17f.

9

guidance on the truth of Christianity, which would soon put an end to that nonsense.'*

Another senior cleric, of another Christian persuasion, took me to his bookshelf where he 'proved' from his books that Moslems worshipped idols called *Termagants*.** He also said that he had read that the Moslems believed that Mohammed's coffin was suspended miraculously in the air but were not allowed to see it***, and that very far from such people being able to surrender to God, their first need was to surrender to truth and save their souls by conversion to Christianity. I don't think he was very pleased when I decided to answer him on his own level and said: 'It sounds a most attractive religion, but I am afraid that I will just have to try to surrender to God, since I don't think that the *termagants* will let me accept your deep erudition.'

The purpose of relating these instances to you is to underline the fact that when we are talking about 'Christians' and 'Moslems' we must first make sure that

*To every minus, of course, there is a plus. There is no likelihood that the venerable Bishop who will follow this exposition is capable of any attitude like that of the one whom I quote. And most felicitously, as I write these works, as if to redress the balance, I open an envelope from my local Protestant Vicar, the erudite and much-respected Rev. Johnson. It contains a greeting card for the festival of Idd al-Fitr, marking the end of the Holy month of Ramadan, which falls today.

**This word in Middle English appears in the old romances and is synonymous with a boistrous trouble-maker. *Tergavants*, from Latin *versari*, 'to turn', means—among other things—'to apostatise'. Perhaps at one time this was applied to Christians who became Moslems. It is also noted in Reinaud's *Invasions*, quoted below.

***The rumour in Europe that Mohammed's coffin was suspended by magnetism in the air 'between mountains' was scotched more than 450 years ago: 'And you must know (I tell it you for a truth) there is no coffin of iron or steel, nor lodestone, nor any mountain within four miles'. (*The Travels of Ludovico di Varthema*, 1503–1508, London (The Hakluyt Society) 1863, quoted by Saunders, John L., in *The Muslim World on the Eve of Europe's Expansion* New Jersey (Prentice-Hall) 1966, 116.)

we are talking about people who have an idea, which should be more or less correct, as to what the other is supposed to believe and what he is expected to do as a consequence of that belief. From personal experience and the examination of literature, I feel that we cannot take for granted that a dialogue, without information and perhaps without understanding, is possible between any individuals or groups on all levels. So the prerequisite is information.

There are, indeed, facilities for the instruction of members of various faiths in the beliefs and practices of others, and books are an obvious source. And there are many people, both Moslem and Christian, who have a good grasp of each others' conceptions of surrender to God and other principles. But the widespread existence of bias, misinformation and lack of knowledge, as well as the enshrining in the very languages which we speak of phrases and formulae which maintain and reinforce the age-old prejudices implanted by ignorant or fanatical ideologists, militate against the effectiveness of dialogue, even if they do not exclude it, by the most subtle and one of the most effective of instruments, the subconscious, almost the subliminal, introduction of hostility.

From imperial, economic and ideological causes, many cultures are the inheritors, and hence the prisoners, of attitudes of scorn and disdain for other faiths—outlooks which are not ennobling to anyone; and which I submit, are positive barriers to the carrying out of basic injunctions, whether these be to love one's neighbour as oneself or to respect the beliefs of others—let alone to seek knowledge about them.

And so a major concern may be represented in this fashion:

The ecumenical ideal cannot even be approached without knowledge, of one's own beliefs and those of others; the surrender to God cannot be understood or coexist with refusal to surrender to facts. God may be above facts: but he does not dispute them. How then can man presume to do so?

What do the Moslems think of Jesus, and why do they think in certain ways about his mission, his surrender and his people? A distinguished Christian cleric and worker in the field of comparative religion has recently reminded his English readers* that Jesus is known as al-Sayyed, The Prince, or ' "the Lord" which is a mark of honour. The title al-Sayyid' he continues, 'is used particularly for Muhammad and his descendants, but also for some other great people. In *City of Wrong*, a study of Jerusalem on Good Friday from an orthodox Muslim point of view, the title "the Lord Christ" is regularly used.'

The important place held by Jesus among the world's six hundred million Moslems,** distributed from the Atlantic shores of Morocco in the West to China, the Philippines and Indonesia in the East, and the agreement of both religions about the necessity for surrender to God as the means of salvation, thus makes it comparatively easy for a Moslem to address himself to Christians: the sympathy and the history are already there.

I have the distinct impression, based upon forty years' contact with people of the Christian communities throughout the world, that the reverse process is by no means as easy. The Christian, for reasons which are fairly clear but only infrequently mentioned, finds that he will tend to approach the Moslem as one who is ignorant, astray and in need of saving. Now this attitude is by no means universal, but it is based upon historical

*Parrinder, Dr. G.: *Jesus in the Qur'an*, London (Faber and Faber) 1965, pp. 33f.

**According to some Christian sources, there are 400 million Moslems, Pakistani figures give 650 million, Egyptian ones 750 million.

causes, and I believe that it is only recently that it has been possible for many to set aside, to overcome, these facts in such a way as to imply an attitude of potential understanding.

The Moslem has the advantage that in his holy Book, the Quran, every word of which has the force of divine law for him, it is clearly stated that Christians are the friends of the Moslems, and that they, along with other believers who do right, have the acceptance of God.

As examples of these statements, let me quote briefly from the Quran where it is said:

'Believers, Jews, Sabaeans or Christians—
whoever believes in God and the Last Day and
does what is right—shall have nothing to fear or
to regret' (Chapter 2, 62).

And:

'. . . the nearest in affection to the believers are
those who say "We are Christians". That is because
there are priests and monks among them, and
because they are not arrogant.' (Chapter 2, 136).

The absence of arrogance, either derived from, or the cause of the desire to surrender to God, which is found among Christians, and which is a part of their religion as we understand it, which can underpin a dialogue between us, has often been attenuated and concealed until quite recent times by political and military struggle between the two communities, based upon geopolitics and human ambition of an expansionist nature during a period which lasted for almost a thousand years.

During all this time there have been many instances of co-operation and understanding between Moslems and Christians, and Jesus himself has never ceased to hold the highest possible place in the mind of Islam; but the background of thinking in Christendom about Islam, with the possible exception of the Christian communities in Moslem lands, has hardly ever, until recently, considered the possibility that Moslems might take any part in the rethinking of religious matters in any sense which might be of interest to, let alone of any value to, Christians.

The dramatic change which has taken place in this attitude in recent years is reflected in the increasing number of writings by men of importance in the West who have begun to consider this possibility, and also, equally important, the far greater currency of these ideas. To write is not enough; the words must be read. To read is not enough, it must be understood.

'... in modern times' says Dr. Geoffrey Parrinder, a major contemporary in the academic study of the comparison of religions*, 'a great deal of re-thinking of traditional doctrines and their expression is being done, so that dialogue between the religions is much easier than for centuries past. Some doctrines, at least, have been expressed in language that is out-dated and often incomprehensible. ... Ideas that Christ came from "up there", "intervened" in the world, and played a super-human role, may need changing to fit conceptions of God as ever-present

*Professor of the Comparative Study of Religions at London University, a Protestant Minister and Secretary of the British Branch of the International Association for the History of Religions.

in the world and of Jesus as fully human and historical. Islam may share with Christianity in this process of rethinking.'*

Individual friendships between Christians and Moslems have been a part of our common history and cultural life for almost fourteen centuries. The effects of these, most of them probably undocumented, continue and must have the most important role in dialogue and mutual understanding. The following instance, found in a general-circulation book of reminiscences with an enormous world sale, is quoted because it is typical, rather than as an occasion for special remark:

The Italian duke Alberto Denti di Pirajno, who lived for many years as a doctor in Islamic countries of the Arabs and Africa, writes of the deep affection between the Apostolic Vicar, in Libya, and the Mayor of Tripoli.

The Bishop 'knew every detail of the life of Mohy ed-Din ben Arabi, a famous Arab mystic of about the year 1200, of whom I had never heard.'

He continues: 'The friendship between the Bishop and the Pasha was one of the most extraordinary I have ever seen. I have never met two men who were, on the surface, more directly opposed in temperament, and rarely have I come across a deeper and closer friendship. The Italian was of modest origin, the Arab the head of a princely family which had once ruled the country; the Bishop held to the simple and pure faith of St. Francis of Assisi, the prince was a fervent and practising Mohammedan; the humble Christian had an encyclopaedic erudition, the Moslem nobleman was

*Parrinder, Dr. Geoffrey: *Jesus in the Qur'an* London (Faber and Faber) 1965, p. 170.

illiterate. .... I had often asked the Bishop about his friendship with the Pasha, endeavouring in my curiosity to discover on what it was based. He was always evasive in his reply; sometimes he did not reply at all, and confined himself to raising his shoulders and blowing into his beard.

'The more I came to know the Arab nobleman, however, the more I discovered what they had in common—for example their indifference to illness, their complete disregard of material considerations, their deep understanding of human suffering and misery, and their charity, which was unsmirched by egotism and knew no limits. Both of them submitted to a higher will with the blind faith of children.

'At a certain point I realized that, just as the various elements in a mosaic form a single design when placed together, so the mental attitudes of the two friends were part of a single spiritual conception which I was at last able to recognize.'

The Duke continues that he at last told the Bishop that he had decided that their friendship was a friendship between Franciscans ... and the Franciscan replied 'I have learnt much from this man.' Pirajno continues:

'The younger of the two friends died first.

'Suddenly the uncertain equilibrium of his metabolism was shaken and the Bishop who had remained a simple friar collapsed.

'I was far away from Tripoli when it happened, and only later did I learn how the Apostolic Vicar had died serenely, surrounded by *confrères* and nuns, gripping the hand of his old friend the Pasha who in his sorrow seemed turned to stone; while in the cathedral, in the mosque, and in the synagogue men of different creeds prayed that God would postpone the appointed hour.'*

Now this account represents the relationship of two men of God, meeting, living and working in what we might call the intermediate period; the post-Crusades era, but yet the time of colonialist rule of a Moslem country, under circumstances which, one might be forgiven for thinking, mutual understanding between members of the ruled and allies of the ruling Power would be extremely difficult. An outside observer might well conclude that, after the colonialist period the beliefs of the occupying power would be discredited, to say the least. And yet today, in independent Libya, as anywhere else in the World of Islam, you may speak a single word against Jesus only at your peril. The teachings of Islam, that Jesus came from God and invited people to surrender to God, are part of the knowledge of every Moslem. Note the following passages from the Qur'an:

'God giveth thee tidings of a word from Him,
whose name is the Messiah, Jesus, son of Mary'
(3, 40–45).

And in Chapter 2, verse 103:

'Say: "We believe in God, and that which hath
been sent down to us, and that which hath been
sent down to Abraham and Ishmael and Isaac and
Jacob and the tribes: and that which hath been
given to Moses and to Jesus, and that which was
given to the Prophets from their Lord. No difference
do we make between any of them: and to God are
we resigned." '

*Alberto Denti Di Pirajno, *A Cure for Serpents*, London (Consul) 1965, 124, 128, 131, 132. (A Book Society Recommendation originally published in Britain in 1955 by André Deutsch.)

The mutal influence of the practice of submission to God, the influence of the practice itself, it might almost be said, upon man has such extensive expressions and has left its mark so deeply that instances are very widespread.

We can even find a typical example, and there may be more than one, in the extremely scanty documentation of the history of Moslem rule in Switzerland, nearly six hundred years before the foundation of this venerable University.

It concerns the devout St. Mayeul, the Abbot of the Monastery of Cluny in Burgundy, and his encounter with the Moslems here: 'Such was the respect in which qualities compelled people to hold him that his name was once seriously mentioned for the high and exalted office of the Papacy.'*

The saint had been on a pilgrimage to Rome, and on his way back was captured by the Moslems, who dominated the countryside. He was held prisoner in a cave, and the Moslems, 'touched by the unalterable calm of the prisoner . . . sought to make his lot a little better. Thus when he required some food, one of them, after washing his hands, prepared a little paste on his shield, cooked it and handed it over to him with great respect and consideration.' One of his captors reminded another that he should respect the Bible which the Abbot carried with him, as the Book of Jesus.**

The Abbot was ransomed by the monks of Cluny and set free by his Saracen captors, and this anecdote is still remembered: though it happened in the year 972 of the Christian reckoning. It is retold in a book reissued by a

*Sherwani's translation of Reinaud's *Invasions* (1836) Ashraf (Lahore, Pakistan) 2nd edition, 1964, pp. 161–4.
**ibid.

Moslem publisher and read in Islamic countries, whose latest edition is dated 1964. Thus does the basis of dedication resound down the centuries, without diminution—for a thousand years.

The submission to the will of God, or Surrender to God, has for Moslems a social and administrative equivalence. Since the Qur'an enjoins certain forms of behaviour, of conduct of state, and the cultivation of moral virtues, these are (for the Moslem) requirements of God: and hence their discharge constitutes surrender to God in the fullest sense. Christian virtues, too, have been expressed in the same way and for similar reasons. We are often reminded that much Western law is based on this concept.

Rainaud's French work about Islamic communities in Europe (including Switzerland, where Moslem suzerainty from its centre in Fraxinet in Provence lasted for many decades) notes the respect which was felt for the achievements and character of the Saracens who ruled so much of Europe. While many clerics regarded these Moslems as pagans and idolaters, the troubadours and poets speak of them with astonishing respect and approval.

Rainaud says that if the Moslem rulers (some of whom were certainly in occupation at Geneva) were to come back to life, they 'would be utterly shocked to find the great changes which have occurred in the respective positions of the Muslims and Christians in Europe; but when the first impressions have been obliterated they would be agreeably surprised at the important place given to their exploits by the old romance-writers of France; and as their spirit would be accustomed to great and adventurous deeds, it would surely pay homage to the sentiment of courtesy which ennobled the barbaric manners of ancient Europeans, and which now seems, alas, to be disappearing day after day.'*

Feelings of respect, and interest in an allied system have not been one-sided. In the popular, narrative and lighter areas of oral admonition, it has been customary for Moslems and Christians to take each others' virtues as texts for teaching. There is a half-humorous tale told among Moslems of the Moslem who asked a Christian why he did not embrace Islam. The Christian said: 'There are two Islams; the one which you practice, and the Islam of the Qur'an. If I were to try to live up to the Qur'an, it would be too difficult for me, for it requires man to make tremendous efforts to improve himself, and I could not receive any absolution from any man, as a Moslem.'

'But' said the Moslem, 'what about the Islam that you call the other kind of Islam—that which I practise?'

'If I were to behave like you do,' said the Christian, 'with your low standards of honesty, I would not be improved, I would be *reduced* in merit.'

The same role of measuring oneself against the other man is found in abundant use among Christians. Thus, from the early days of the confrontation between the two religions, Christians are frequently on record as contrasting, in approach to their flocks, the achievements, industry, piety and so on of the Moslems, as against their own current conduct. They generally even attribute the worldly success of the Moslems of their times to their having practised, that is, submitted them-

*Invasions des Sarrazins en France, et de France en Savoie, en Piemont et en Suisse, translated by Haroon Khan Sherwani, Lahore (Ashraf) 1964 edition, p. 239.

selves to, the ordinances of God which concern the cultivation of such direct and derivative commands as truthfulness, honesty and dedication to ideals.

4

One of the earliest parts of Islamic history—the emigration of the persecuted to Abyssinia—contains in full measure clear indications of a strong appreciation of, and gratitude for, the surrender to God as being essential and, where circumstances require it, total, come what may. Ninety-four Moslem families had emigrated to Abyssinia by 615 A.D., five years after Mohammed's first call.

In early Islamic history, a most dramatic and widely-studied part of the development of the community of the Moslems concerns the dialogue, co-operation and understanding between two extraordinarily important communities, one Moslem, the other Christian, which illustrates the appreciation by a far-sighted and noble Christian king of people who surrender to the will of God, and the consequent preservation of a significant portion of the infant community of Islam. This concerns the sheltering and encouragement of the early Moslem refugees from the idolaters by the Christian king of Ethiopia.

The most ancient Islamic histories, embodied in the authoritative Life of the Prophet, Ibn Ishaq's *Sirat Rasul Allah* (Life of the Messenger of God), goes into considerable detail on this determining event, quoting verbatim from the survivors.

During the early days of Mohammed's preaching, his followers were subjected to severe persecution by the Meccans, notably by the tribe of Quraish, guardians of the idol-house. 'Then the Quraysh showed their enmity to all those who followed the apostle; every clan which contained Muslims attacked them, imprisoning them, and beating them, allowing them no food or drink, and

23

exposing them to the burning heat of Mecca....'
Abdullah ibn Abbas reported: 'They used to beat one
of them, depriving him of food and drink so that he
could hardly sit upright because of the violence they
had used on him, so that in the end he would do whatever they said....'

Mohammed advised his followers to go to the Christian land of Abyssinia, saying, 'The king will not
tolerate injustice.'*

Now the Quraish sent costly presents with two of
their representatives to Abyssinia to secure the return
of the Moslems, who meanwhile had been received
kindly by the Negus and allowed to practise their
religion.**

These ambassadors went to the generals of the Negus
and said:

'Some foolish fellows from our people have taken
refuge in the King's country. They have forsaken our
religion and not accepted yours, but have brought in
an invented religion, which neither you nor we know
anything about. Our nobles have sent us to the King
to get him to return them.' The generals agreed to
report to the King, and took him the presents, which he
accepted. They advised the Negus to surrender the
refugees, without examination, saying that the poly-
theists knew best about the character of their own
people.

'The Negus was enraged and said, "No, by God, I
will not surrender them. No people who have sought
my protection, settled in my country, and chosen me
rather than others shall be betrayed, until I summon

*This and other extracts from Professor A. Guillaume's English transla-
tion, Oxford (University Press) 1955, 146. Ibn Ishaq died 767 A.D.
**Ibid., 150.

24

them and ask them about what these two men al-
allege. ...." Then he summoned the Apostle's com-
panions, and when his messenger came they gathered
together, saying to one another, "What will you say to
the man when you come to him?". They said, "We
shall say what we know, and what our Prophet commanded, come what may". When they came into the
royal presence they found that the king had summoned
his bishops with their sacred books exposed around
him. He asked them what was the religion for which
they had forsaken their people, without entering into
his religion or any other. Ja'far b. Abu Talib answered,
'O King, we were an uncivilized people, worshipping
idols, eating corpses, committing abominations, breaking natural ties, treating guests badly, and our strong
devoured our weak. Thus we were until God sent us an
apostle whose lineage, truth, trustworthiness, and
clemency we know. He summoned us to acknowledge
God's unity and to worship him and to renounce the
stones and images which we and our fathers formerly
worshipped. He commanded us to speak the truth, be
faithful to our engagements, mindful of the ties of
kinship and kindly hospitality, and to refrain from
crimes and bloodshed. He forbade us to commit
abominations and to speak lies, and to devour the
property of orphans, to vilify chaste women, He commanded us to worship God alone and not to associate
anything with Him, and he gave us orders about prayer,
almsgiving and fasting. ...."

One of the Moslems, at the King's request, then read
a passage from the nineteenth chapter of the Quran.

'The Negus wept until his beard was wet and the
bishops wept until their scrolls were wet. . . . Then the
Negus said, "Of a truth, this and what Jesus brought

have come from the same niche. You two may go, for, by God, I will never give them up to them and they shall not be betrayed." '*

In Ethiopia today, according to the International Year Book and Statesmen's Who's Who** one-third of the population is pagan, one-third Christian and the remaining third Moslem.

*Ibid., 151f.

**London (Burke's Peerage) 1971 edition, p. 199. Official population estimate: 23 million (Ibid., p. 197). Estimates vary between 15 and 28 million. One gives a total of 21·8 million, with 13·08 million as Moslems (World Muslim Gazeteer, Karachi (World Muslim Congress) 1964, p. 558.

5

The nearness of the Moslems to the Christians, and especially to those who adopted the devotional life, and hence the respect felt by Moslems for those who surrender to God, is emphasized by the Charter granted to the monks of the Monastery of St. Catherine, near Mount Sinai, which is a statement of the attitude of Islam, given by Mohammed himself, and an important historical document, dating from 627 A.D.:

'By it the Prophet secured to the Christians important privileges and immunities, and the Moslems were prohibited under severe penalties from violating and abusing what was therein ordered. In this charter the Prophet undertook himself, and enjoined his followers, to protect the Christians, to guard them from all injuries, and to defend their churches, and the residences of their priests. They were not to be unfairly taxed; no bishop was to be driven out of his bishopric; no Christian was to be forced to reject his religion; no monk was to be expelled from his monastery; no pilgrim was to be detained from his pilgrimage; nor were the Christian churches to be pulled down for the sake of building mosques or houses for the Moslems. Christian women married to Moslems were to enjoy their own religion, and not to be subjected to compulsion or annoyance of any kind on that account. If the Christians should stand in need of assistance for the repair of their churches or monasteries, or any other matter pertaining to their religion, the Moslems were to assist them.'*

*Ameer Ali, Syed, *A Short History of the Saracens*, London (Macmillan) 1949 edition, pp. 14f.

6

But the Christian connexion with Islam dates from an even earlier period; from a time, indeed, when some pre-Islamic Arabs were seeking the *Hanifi* faith, the name locally given to the religion of surrender to God of Abraham, their progenitor, and when Christians were found among the Arabs of the Hejaz,* as well as in the more northernly lands of Syria, where there are still most flourishing Churches, of over half a million Christians out of a population of 5 million.

Spiritually and culturally, the world of Islam has a most powerful continuing link with Christianity through the Lebanon, one of the most progressive Arab countries, whose population has a majority of Christians, and whose President is, by custom, always a member of the Christian faith. The Maronites number almost double all other religious groups, the remainder of the Christians being mainly Orthodox and Greek Catholic.**

This aspect of our common history, bound up with the seekers of truth, pagan, Zoroastrian and Christian, of those times, entitles us to think in terms of an alliance of attitude which present-day conditions make it possible to invoke and to examine, as some Christians are now examining it, as I shall mention in a moment.

It was a Christian monk, according to Islamic tradition, who first informed the polytheist Arabs

---

*There were Arab kings and large churches, and bishops, in pre-Islamic times in Arabia: and whole tribes are said to have been Christians. (Cf. Sale, *The Koran*, Preliminary Discourse, quoting Al-Mustatraf, Ahmad b. Yusuf, Safiuddin, etc.).

**The Middle East & North Africa*, London (Europa) 1969, p. 449.

among whom Mohammed was being brought up, that he was to become a spiritual teacher. Mohammed was at that time twelve years old, and his mission was not to begin for another twenty-eight years.

Now for the next important historical occasion.

When the Mecca trading caravan of Abu Talib, uncle of Mohammed, was moving towards its Syrian destination, it passed the Christian monastery of Jabal Harun, where a certain revered Christian monk, Bahira, worshipped, performing his devotions and dedicating his life to God.

One day, breaking his ordinary custom, Bahira, to the perplexity of the caravaneers, invited them all to a feast at his monastery.

Bahira did not explain his reasons to them, but looked at them all, one by one, and then asked:

'Is there any one of your number who did not accompany you tonight?'

'Yes', they said, 'there is one, a young lad of twelve years of age, whom we left in our tents below, too young to accompany us.'*

Bahira insisted that he be brought and said to him: 'Young man, I have a question to ask—will you answer it, by Lat and Uzza, your great gods of stone?'

The youth answered:

'Do not address me in the name of idols, for I owe no allegiance to them: but ask me in the name of God, and by God I shall answer you.'

Bahira asked him many things, and finally turned to Abu Talib and said:

'This is no ordinary man, this Mohammed, thy brother's son. He shall be a prophet. Heed my words and watch over him with constant care, thy charge is precious to humanity.'**

*Mohammed was born on 29 August, 570 of the Christian Era.

**Shah, Sirdar Ikbal Ali, *Mohammed: The Prophet*, London, (Wright and Brown) first edition 1932, 91f.

It was nearly three decades later, at the most important occasion of Mohammed's life, that another Christian, an Arab, devout and well versed in the scriptures, a man who had sought the Hanifite path, entered his life. This was in the year 610 A.D., when Mohammed, in the Cave on Mount Hira, received his first spiritual experience, and feared that he had gone mad or become—as he said—a poet. When the voice addressed him, he went to his wife in Mecca, trembling with fear, saying, 'Woe is me, poet or possessed!'. He had even thought of casting himself down from the high rocks to kill himself. Mohammed thought that people would never believe what he had to say, but she reminded him that he was of impeccable character, and was known by the title of Al-Amin, the Truthful.

She took her husband at once to her cousin, Waraqah son of Nofal, the devout Christian, for his advice. Waraqah heard the account of the voice and what it had said, and cried out:

'By the Most Holy God! If what thou hast said is true, this is the voice of the Angel who appeared to Moses. . . . Doubt me not, thy husband, Khadija, is the Prophet risen out of the Tribe of the Quraish. . . .' And he said to Mohammed, 'Would that I were to be in the land of the living when thy kinsmen send thee into exile . . . whoever brings what thou bringest falls victim to a most dastardly persecution.'*

The voice had said, preserved in the Qur'an (74, 1ff):
'O Thou, enwrapped in thy mantle!
Arise and warn'.

· · · · ·

Ibid., 106–7.

The interchange between Christians and Moslems, marked by the recognition of the overwhelming importance of the concept of submission to the Will of God, has been continuously present for the past fourteen centuries.* Mohammed's words to Bahira at the age of twelve speak of his submission to God alone. Waraqa's welcome of him was based upon his repetition of the injunction of the angel to *obey* God; the Ethiopian King's acceptance of the Moslems was rooted in their account of their efforts to submit, to *surrender*, to those principles which had been preached to them. The dialogue, which we characterise in the title of these discussions as 'An Attempt to Dialogue' starts before the proclamation of Islam, continues through the infancy of Islam and the period of the supremacy of the Moslems in the East, is to be found in the mutual respect during the Crusades,** in Moslem Spain where so very many Christian scholars (including at least one pope, Gerbert)*** studied, and it survived the colonialist period from which we have just emerged. It is to be found both in the writings and speech of contemporary Moslem and Christian thinkers and of

*One has only to read Evelyn Underhill, the authority on Christian mysticism (*The Mystic Way*, London, 1913) to see how she constantly mentions Sufi psychology and its affinity in results with Christian devotion.

**This aspect is, of course, abundantly covered in many books and is a matter of common knowledge. 'When Usman b. Munqidh, a Syrian Amir of thn 12th Century, visited Jerusalem, during a period of truce (in the 2nd Crusade) the Knights Templar, who had occupied the Masjid-al-Aqsa (the Farthest Mosque, near the Dome of the Rock) assigned to him a small chapel adjoining it, for him to say his prayers in, and they strongly resented the interference on the part of a newly-arrived Crusader, who took this new departure in the direction of religious freedom in very bad part'. (Arnold, Sir Thomas: *op. cit.*, (p. 90) quoting Guizot, *Histoire de la Civilisation en Europe*. Paris 1882.

***Sylvester II, 999 A.D., see Hitti, *History of the Arabs*, s.v. Sylvester II.

workers of these communities in the political, economic, scientific and human fields.

Contemporary Western thinkers do not disdain the possibility of understanding still to be developed from thinking such as that of such great intellects and mystics as Al-Ghazzali—of whom we shall have more to say later—in recognition of the common problems which face believers today. 'Islam,' in the words of Professor W. Montgomery Watt of Edinburgh, the distinguished Arabist* is now wrestling with Western thought as it once wrestled with Greek philosophy, and is as much in need as it was then of a 'revival of the religious sciences'. Deep study of Al-Ghazzali may suggest to Muslims steps to be taken if they are to deal successfully with the contemporary situation. Christians, too, now that the world is in a cultural melting-pot, must be prepared to learn from Islam, and are unlikely to find a more sympathetic guide than Al-Ghazzali.'

*Watt, W. Montgomery, *The Faith and Practice of Al-Ghazzali*, London (Allen) 1963, p. 15. Ghazzali died in the year 1111. The allusion is to his book *The Ihya'* (Revival of Religious Sciences) which we quote below.

Now I would like to pause to consider some of the
ways in which Moslems think of Allah, God whom they
worship and to whose will submission, surrender is their
goal. In the words of one of the best-known parts of the
Merciful Qur'an, the Throne Verse:*

Allah! There is no deity but he
The Living, the Eternal Being
No slumber overtakes him
Nor sleep. His is what is in the heavens
And on earth.
Who can intercede with him except with his leave?
He knows all that is before them and after them;
And they have none of his knowledge except what
    he wills
And his throne extends over the heavens
And the earth, and its protection is no burden to
    him
And he is The Most High and The Most Great.

Another of the most-repeated passages, is Sura 24
(The Light), Verse 35, known as the Light Verse,
which refers to God in the analogy of illumination, and
which has been taken by many of the Moslem mystics,
such as Al-Ghazzali** in their attempt to teach the
path of surrender to the will of Allah:

'God is the Light of the Heavens and of the Earth,
His light may be compared to a niche within which
is a lamp: the lamp within a crystal like a star.
It is lit from a blessed olive tree, neither of the
East nor of the West—its very oil would be well-nigh

*Qur'an, Baqara (2): 255. (Throne Verse).

**This is the text upon which Ghazzali's celebrated treatise Mishkat
an-Anwar (The Niche of Lights) is based.

luminous though fire touched it not. Light upon light! Allah guides to his light whom He will.'

These major texts are traditionally those which have been used for contemplation by Moslem mystics who follow the path of surrender.

Stories of Jesus, and references to him, abound in the Quran, in the Traditions of the Prophet, and in the devotional and psychological literature of Islam. Some of these are well known to Christians through their own Gospels; others are less familiar to them. As teacher of salvation through submission, Jesus is often held up as a model. One could write a book, or talk for months, about this aspect of the tradition. But one small sample of how Jesus is cited in Islam as teaching through words and actions, in illustrating on the mortal plane by positive action the rewards of submission to God, I choose this brief extract from Ihya al-Ulum,

The Revival of Religious Sciences: *

'It is narrated that Jesus—on whom be peace—saw a blind leper, who was saying:

"Praise to God, who has saved me from many things which have befallen others."

"From what affliction art thou free?" Jesus asked him·

"Spirit of God", said the leper, "I am better off than those who do not know God."

"You speak truly" said Jesus, "stretch out your hand".

He put out his hand and instantly was restored to perfect health, through the power of God. And he followed Jesus and worshipped with him.'

This demonstration-teaching, as one might name it, may be seen to have an equivalence, whether this be on a lower plane or not, in social action as well as in the

*by Al-Ghazzali, (Vol. 4).

spiritual discipline of which we will speak later. Bring-
ing ourselves right up to the present day, and trans-
posing into an area within our own daily concern and
competence of action, we may note the thought of one
of our contemporary great men who sees no obstacle to
to interpreting 'surrender' in terms of arming ourselves to carry out human missions.

'Surrender to God' must mean a surrender to the
Principles which represent, are derived from and analogous to, those of the highest ideals of that which is good.
This surrender, therefore, can be (and indeed must be)
expressed in social and psychological and other terms,
as well as in distinctly devotional ones confined to
religious specialization within ideological communities,
sects or institutions claiming exclusivity.

An example of this in the social, legal and political
field is given by one of Islam's most distinguished
thinkers and men of action, the statesman Abd al-
Rahman Azzam Pasha,* whose name and thought are
known and respected throughout Islam:

'It is our right, we, the descendants of just, equitable
and merciful people in the East, as Muslims and as
Christians, to strive for a rebirth in which we shall
serve as examples and spokesmen for freedom of
belief and of opinion in a world that has become
tolerant of those who differ in their views. Our fore-
fathers were the protectors of this freedom and its
supreme example. Let us inherit this tolerance, and let
us bear its standard.'

In this sense, the service of man *is* the service of God,
and discharging our duty to man *is* fulfilling God's

*In *The Eternal Message of Muhammad*, New York (Mentor) 1965,
p. 175.

37

commands, and hence surrendering to what he has commanded us to do.*

In this sense, too, the dialogue is already in being: for Moslems and Christians already work together throughout the world, though not everywhere or always, on tasks which are rooted in an acceptance of the commands of God to all; and hence in surrender.

This can, of course, only be a voluntary task, which can never be imposed; imposition of service, in the sense in which Moslems and Christians alike understand it, is an absurdity, an impossibility. Islam, the very word meaning 'Submission' means freedom and choice in service in its perceptible as well as in its interior senses. This is so important that it is written in a famous passage in the Quran, which of course has the force of law for all Moslems:

'Wilt thou compel men to become believers? No soul can believe but by the leave of God.'**

And, perhaps even more familiar, at least to Moslems, is the command:

'Let there be no compulsion in religion.'***

*One of the great Islamic mystic authors, the classical Persian poet Saadi, says in a famous passage:

'The Way is not otherwise than in the service of the people. It is not in rosaries and prayer rugs and robes'. *Bostan*, I.

**10, 99–100.

***2, 257.

II

I have been asked, by a great Western orientalist (who has also asked me not to name him) that, as I shall be dealing with dialogue between Christians and Moslems, he feels that it is incumbent upon me to denounce—as he puts it—the scorn which some Moslem scholars have from time to time directed towards European and American orientalists and other specialists. He also writes that I should make it plain that, in his estimation, one cannot speak of, or for, 'Moslems' as a whole, since they are grouped into two main sections, the Sunni and the Shia'h, and that therefore, he believes, there can be no dialogue between Moslems as such and Christians as such. And that Sufis, mystics of Islam, though surrendering to God, are in fact anti-Moslem.

I beg your indulgence to deal with these points. Ordinarily one would not have given them much prominence, but after contacting a number of Christian scholars who have made Islam their study, I have discovered from their reactions that they, too, feel that this is a fit subject for emphasis.

When the Prophet Mohammed was asked to curse unbelievers, he replied, according to authoritative tradition, 'I was not sent for this, nor was I sent but as a mercy to mankind.' He further said: 'It is unworthy to injure people's reputations; and it is unworthy to curse anyone; and it is unworthy to abuse anyone; and it is unworthy for the Faithful to talk vainly.'

As to the matter of whether we speak as Moslems, in spite of what has been called the difference between Shiahs and Sunnis, I do not myself believe that it is necessary to attempt to compose answers when this has already been sufficiently well done. The Moslems follow the precept laid down by Mohammed when he said: 'Moslems are like one wall, some parts strengthening others; in such a way they must support each other.'

Following the reasoning that something which has been well and adequately said should be repeated rather than an attempt made to supplant it, I am fortunate to be able to quote from a recent comment upon this subject by a great scholar of Islam in Persia, Seyyed Hossein Nasr, who is Professor of the History of Science and Philosophy in Tehran, and comes from an honoured family. In a book recently published in the West he says:

'In fact, Sunnism and Shi'ism, belonging both to the total orthodoxy of Islam, do not in any way destroy its unity. The unity of a tradition is not destroyed by different applications of it but by the destruction of its principles and forms as well as its continuity. Being 'the religion of unity' Islam, in fact, displays more homogeneity and less religious diversity than other worldwide religions.'*

Within the 'submission system' of Islam, as in Christi-

*Nasr, Seyyid Hossein, *Ideals and Realities of Islam*, London (George Allen & Unwin) 1966 (1971 impression), p. 148.

anity, there is room for a tremendous variety of opinion, once the basic beliefs are accepted. The basic of Islam is submission to God, but there have been (indeed still are) Moslems who accept the Quran as the law and not the Traditions, the 'Sayings' of the Prophet. There are even those who call the *Sharia*, commonly accepted as the Holy Way of Law or Islam in its extrapolation from the Quran, an 'innovation'. The basic commandment is so basic that this diversity in unity is possible. Moslem thinkers themselves sometimes express surprise when they come across varieties of this phenomenon, though they seldom fail to integrate examples into their thought when time has done its work. And this has always been the way in Islam.

As for the misconception of Sufis as mad dervishes, opportunists and mountebanks, or mysterious at best, degenerate at worst, undermining Islam, faith and social stability, cultists of doubtful habits and exploiting tendencies, imitators of saints, this is by no means confined to the West. But since the explanation is simple (that there are rotten apples possible in any barrel and Sufis' utterances are not always understood without context) and plenty of people have helped to right the record down the centuries, what is needed is only information on a wide scale: and understanding— and only those lacking one or more of these really remain opposed, the outlook for Sufi knowledge and appreciation of the past, present and future Sufi contribution is bright indeed. Professor Nasr has illuminated many important aspects of this picture for Western scholars, and he may have been hard done by through the publication of criticism of his work which alleges emotional bias and anti-Western subjectivity. He has, in fact, generously acknowledged much Western work of Sufism, Shiahism, comparative religion and various ways of looking at metaphysics.*

*In, for instance, *Sufi Essays*, London, (George Allen & Unwin) 1972, he covers many interesting points, deplores the activities of superficialists, and imitators, discusses the Shiah and Sunni attitudes, and cites recent Western work which has attempted to convey Sufi thought in Western modes.

12

It should, however, be remembered that the sort of
opposition which a scholar encounters today is rarely
anything like what our next writer, the great mystic
Al-Ghazzali, had to face: with his works thrown into
the flames in Spain by his coreligionists.* Looking at
the 500 entries in a bibliography of references to my
own books, now in preparation, we find that, including
the usual personal attacks and ideological vilification,
less than four per cent are hostile, from all countries;
and some of those at least seem clearly based upon
misunderstandings.

.   .   .   .   .

We have seen how Christians and Moslems have
thought alike and worked together, how they have
respected one anothers' spirituality and service, and
how each has appreciated the concept of surrender
which is inherent in the tradition which links them.

Before going further into the sociology, psychology or
history of the two religions, I want to tell you something
of a typical Moslem approach. Here are the words of
one of our greatest mystics, Al-Ghazzali, (1058–1111)
whose works were so esteemed in the Middle Ages of
Christendom that clerics are on records in the West as
holding the belief that he was in fact a Christian writer,
'sound in doctrine'; whereas Ghazzali was, of course,
not only an experiential Sufi mystic but a former
professor of Islamic theology of the Nizamia at
Baghdad.

In the passages here selected from the *Minhaj al-*

*Who later acclaimed him as 'the Proof of Islam'.

Abidin, ('The Way of the Worshippers', or High Road of the Submitted), he describes experiences and the disciplines which accompany the seeker in his efforts to worship and to fulfil the will of God.

First we may briefly note a Christian scholar's view of him:

'Another writer whose work had great influence on the West was Algazel (Abu Hamid ibn Muhammad al-Tusi Al-Ghazzali, (1058–1111). Surnamed *Hujjatu-l-Islam*, "Islam's convincing Proof", his varied life was lived amid the significant intellectual and religious movements of his day. In turn he had been philosopher, scholastic, traditionist, sceptic and mystic. A man of unquestionable sincerity and firm moral purpose—one of the comparatively few men of his race who consistently exerted himself to awake in his co-religionists a zeal for morality—he has retained in Islam a position somewhat comparable with that of St. Thomas Aquinas in Christianity. In reading his theological treatises one remembers only with an effort that the author is a Muhammadan".*

This is the passage describing the Seven Valleys, written in the eleventh century, and considered a textbook of mystical teaching, derived from Ghazzali's own experience:

THE SEVEN VALLEYS

Know, my brethren, that worship is the fruit of knowledge, the benefit of life and the capital of virtues. It is the aim and object of men of noble aspirations to have keen inward sight. It is their *summum bonum* and their

---

*Prof. Alfred Guillaume, 'Philosophy and Theology', in *Legacy of Islam*, pp. 269f (Oxford 1968 printing).

everlasting Paradise. 'I am your Creator', says the Quran. 'Worship Me. You will have your recompense and your efforts will be rewarded.'

Worship then is essential for man but it is beset with difficulties and hardships. It has stumbling blocks and pitfalls in its tortuous path which is haunted by cut-throats and goblins while helpers are scarce and friends are few. But this path of worship must be dangerous, for says the Prophet, 'Paradise is surrounded by sufferings and covered by tribulations, while Hell abounds in ease and free enjoyment of passions. Poor man! he is weak, his engagements are heavy: times are hard and life is short. But journey from here to hereafter being unavoidable, if he neglects taking necessary provisions he is sure to perish. Ponder over the gravity of the situation and the seriousness of our condition. By Allah our lot is pitiable indeed, for many are called but few are chosen.

When I found the path of worship so difficult and dangerous I composed certain works, chiefly *Ihya ulum-iddin* in which I pointed out the ways and means of surmounting those difficulties, facing the dangers boldly and crossing the path with success. But certain persons looking to the outward expressions of my work failed to understand the meaning and purpose of it and not only rejected the book* but treated it in a manner unbecoming of a Muslim. But I was not disheartened for there were persons who used to ridicule the Holy Quran calling it "The Stories of the Ancients". Nor was I offended for I felt pity on them for they knew not what they were doing to themselves. I hate disputations now but I must do something for them. So out of

*During the lifetime of the author the book was publicly burnt in the market by the Ulama of Spain, the land of Inquisition.

compassion for my brethren I prayed to God to enlighten me on the subject in a new manner.

Listen, then, that the first requisite which awakens man from the lethargy of forgetfulness and turns him towards the path, is God's grace which stirs the mind to meditate thus:

I am the recipient of so many gifts—life, power, reason, speech—and I find myself mysteriously protected from many troubles and evils. Who is my benefactor? Who is my saviour? I must be grateful to him in a fitting manner otherwise the gifts will be taken away and I shall be undone. These gifts reveal their purpose like tools in the hands of an artisan and the world appears to me like a beautiful picture leading my thoughts towards the painter.

i The Valley of Knowledge

The soliloquy takes him to the Valley of Knowledge where implicit faith in the Divine Messenger leads the way and tells him:

The Benefactor is that One Being who has no associate with Him. He is thy Creator who is omnipresent though unseen, whose Commandments must be obeyed both inwardly and outwardly. He has so ordained that the good shall be rewarded and the wicked punished. The choice is now thine for thou are held responsible for thy actions. Acquire knowledge under God-fearing *Ulama** with a conviction that knows no wavering.

When the Valley of Knowledge is crossed man prepares for worship, but his guilty conscience upbraids him saying, 'Canst thou knock at the door of the Sanctuary? Away with thy pollutious abominations!'

*Learned men.

46

ii The Valley of Repentance

The poor sinner falls down in the Valley of Repentance when a voice is heard, 'Repent, repent! for thy Lord is Forgiving'. He now takes heart and rising with joy proceeds further.

iii The Valley of Stumbling Blocks

And he enters into a Valley full of stumbling blocks chief of which are four in number, *viz.*, the tempting world; the attracting people; the old enemy Satan and the inordinate self. Let him have four counter-forces so as to tide over the difficulty. Try to choose retired life; avoid mixing with all sorts of people; fight out the old enemy and control thyself by the bridle of piety.

Let it be remembered that the fourfold counter-forces have to face four other psychological troubles, *viz.*, (1) Anxious care about man's daily bread as a result of his retirement. (2) Doubts and anxieties about his private affairs disturbing peace of his mind. (3) Worries, hardships and indignities for want of social contact. For when man wishes to serve his God, Satan attacks him openly and secretly from all sides. (4) Unpleasant happenings and unexpected sufferings as the outcome of his destiny.

iv The Valley of Tribulations

These psychological troubles throw the poor worshipper into the Valley of Tribulations. In this plight let man protect himself by (1) Dependence on God in the matter of his sustenance. (2) Invocation of His help when he finds himself helpless. (3) Patience in sufferings. (4) Joyous submission to His Will.

v The Thundering Valley

Crossing this fearful Valley of Tribulations man thinks that the passage will not be easy but to his amazement he finds that service is uninteresting, prayers are mechanical and contemplation has no pleasure. He is indolent, melancholy and stupid. Puzzled and perplexed he now enters into the Thundering Valley. The lightning flash of Hope dazzles his sight and he falls down trembling when he hears the deafening sound of the thunder of Fear. His eyes brimming with tears imitate the clouds and his pure thoughts flash with the lightning. In a moment the mystery of Human Responsibility with its reward for good actions and punishment for wicked deeds was solved. Henceforth his worship will not be lip service and his daily work will not be a drudgery. Soaring on high he will ply on the wings of Hope and Fear.

vi The Abysmal Valley

With a light heart, in a happy mood, he was now proceeding further when suddenly the Abysmal Valley presents its dreadful sight. Looking deep into the nature of his actions he found that those who were good were either actuated by the desire of winning the approbation of his fellow men or were simply the outcome of vainglory. On one side he saw the hydra-headed monster of hypocrisy lurking and on the other side the bewitching Pandora of Conceit with her box open. In despair he knew not what to do when, lo! the Angel of Sincerity emerged from the depth of his heart and taking him by the arm carried him through the valley.

Expressing his gratitude for the Divine favour he was proceeding further when the thought of multifarious favours for his unworthy self and his incapacity to do full justice to his thanksgivings overwhelmed him.

vii The Valley of Hymns

This was the Valley of Hymns where, mortal as he was, he tried his best to sing the songs of praise to the Immortal Being. The Invisible Hand of Divine Mercy then opened the door of the Garden of Love, he was ushered in with body and soul for both had played their part directly and indirectly. Here ends the Journey. The worshipper is now living among his fellow men like a traveller but his heart lives in Him waiting to carry out the last order, 'O soul thou art at peace! return to thy Creator well-pleased, well pleasing. Then enter among My Servants and enter into My Paradise.' (Quran, ch. LXXXIX, al-Fajr.)*

.   .   .   .   .

*Vide: Ali, Syed Nawab, *Some Moral and Religious Teachings of Al-Ghazzali*, Baroda (1920) and Lahore (Ashraf), 1960, 3rd. edition, pp. 159ff.

13

The study methods of surrender, of contemplation and abstinence, of the Christian and Moslem surrenderers to God, not only commanded the assent of devotees of both persuasions—as instance Lully's approval of the Sufis and their recitations—but produced a common result,—and even, as in the following passages, an almost mysterious identity between some of the greatest Christian and Islamic mystics.

It is worth recalling several instances, and certain patterns, of the interaction and relationship between Moslems and Christians, as recorded in readily-available form. Some of the accounts, such as those of Saladin and the Crusaders, or the influence of common searches for knowledge in Arabised Spain, are widely known to readers of all kinds of literature, and even to many who watch films or television documentary programmes. Other events and developments are mainly known only in local cultures; and these include the life of Roderigo 'the Cid' (el-Saiyid), and the story of the Christians who fought side by side with the Moslems against the Persian oppressors in the early years of Islam. But there is so much other material, both narrative and literary, that looking through it one could almost call it a pattern, or a series of patterns. I have chosen one or two instances and themes to indicate what I mean.

One of the Moslem spiritual teachers best known in the West is, of course, Jalaluddin Rumi (1207–73), the mystic and poet who had Christian and Jewish, as well as Moslem, followers. We can begin with an account, preserved in Aflaki's *Munaqib al-Arifin** (The Acts of the

*Redhouse, James W. *Legends of the Sufis*, Kingston, 1965 (reprint of the 1881 edition 'The Acts of the Adepts').

Adepts) about the Persian merchant who sought wisdom and whom Rumi taught by a striking object lesson.

This man of Tabriz came to Qonya (Asiatic Turkey, then known as Roum) in search of spiritual teaching, and brought with him fifty sequins as an offering. Aflaki, translated by Redhouse, continues:

'When they reached the college, Jelal was sitting alone in the lecture-hall, immersed in the study of some books. The party made their obeisances, and the merchant felt himself completely overpowered at the aspect of the venerable teacher; so that he burst into tears, and could not utter a word. Jelal addressed him, therefore, as follows:

"The fifty sequins thou hast provided as thy offering are accepted. . . . The cause and reason of thy bygone losses"—about which the merchant was concerned—"was, that, on a certain day thou wast in the west of Farangistan (Europe), where thou wentest into a certain ward of a certain city, and there sawest a poor Farangi (European) man, one of the greatest of God's cherished saints, who was lying stretched out at the corner of a market-place. As thou didst pass him by, thou spattest on him, evincing aversion from him. His heart was grieved by thy act and demeanour. Hence the visitations that have afflicted thee. Go thou, then, and make thy peace with him, asking his forgiveness, and offering him our salutations."

'The merchant was petrified at this announcement. Jelal then asked him: "Wilt thou that we this instant show him to thee?" So saying, he placed his hand on the wall of the apartment, and told the merchant to behold. Instantly, a doorway opened in the wall, and the merchant thence perceived that man in Farangistan lying down in a market-place. At this sight he bowed down his head and rent his garments, coming away from the saintly presence in a state of stupor. He remembered all these incidents as facts.

'Immediately commencing his preparations, he set out without delay, and reached the city in question. He enquired for the ward he wished to visit, and for the man whom he had offended. Him he discovered lying down, stretched out as Jelal had shown him. The merchant dismounted from his beast, and made his obeisance to the prostrate Farangi dervish, who at once addressed him thus: "What wilt that I do? Our Lord Jelal suffereth me not; or otherwise, I had a desire to make thee see the power of God, and what I am. But now, draw near."

'The Farangi dervish then clasped the merchant to his bosom, kissed him repeatedly on both cheeks, and then added: "Look now, that thou mayest see my Lord and Teacher, my spiritual Master, and that thou mayest witness a marvel." The merchant looked. He saw the Lord Jelal immersed in holy dance, chanting this hymn, and entranced with sacred music:

"His kingdom's vast and pure; each sort its fitting
place finds there;
Cornelian, ruby, clod, or pebble be thou on His
hill.
Believe, He seeks thee; disbelieve, He'll haply
cleanse thee fair;
Be here a faithful Abu-Bekr;* Farangi there; at
will." '

It is also related that when Jalal died, the 'mourners

*i.e., Orthodox observer of the majority persuasion in Islam; hence contrasted with a Western Christian. It has been asserted that the 'Frankish dervish' was none other than Ramon Lull ('Raymond Lully') of Majorca, whose writings speak approvingly of the Sufis.

were of all creeds, and of various nations; Jews and Christians, Turks, Romans and Arabians were among them. Each recited sacred passages, according to their several usages, from the Law, the Psalms, or the Gospel. The Muslims strove to drive away these strangers. They would not be repelled. A great tumult was the result. The Sultan, the Heir-Apparent, and the Perwana all flew to appease the strife, together with the chief Rabbis, the Bishops, Abbots, &c.

'It was asked of these latter' continues the legend, 'why they mixed themselves up with the funeral of an eminent Muslim sage and saint. They replied that they had learnt from him more of the mysteries shrouded in their scriptures, than they had ever known before; and had found in him all the signs and qualities of a prophet and saint, as set forth in those writings. They further declared: "If you Muslims hold him to have been the Muhammad of his age, we esteem him as the Moses, the David, the Jesus of our time; and we are his disciples, his adherents." The Muslim leaders could make no answer. . . . He had died as the sun went down on the 16th December 1273,' at sixty-six solar years of age. *

Although Al-Ghazzali's delineation of the psychic geography of the Valleys which we have looked at does not depend for its impact on any knowledge of the Arabic language; and Rumi did not work primarily in Arabic, but Persian, yet the influence and inner dimensions of Arabic have always had an importance in the interaction between those whose mother-tongue it is, whether they be Moslems or Christians.

So I propose to return to this aspect of the understanding of the concept of 'Surrender', to throw what

*Op. cit., p. 96.

additional light we can upon it in the interests of Christian-Moslem understanding.

Al-Ghazzali, though born at Tus, in what was known as Khurasan, Eastern Persia, near the Holy City of Mashad, used, for the most part, the Arabic language which was also at that time equally well known to the Eastern (Arabian) Christians and very many of the outstanding Christians of Latin Europe, through their contact with, and study in, the Spanish-Arabian schools. The use of Arabic was an important element in the mutual understanding between Christians and Moslems in many areas of belief and practice, significantly because whole plethoras of meanings, related to the same stem or root, could be deduced by the use of an Arabic word which showed the relationship of concepts which, when translated into other tongues, lost their inevitable associations.

In order to bring this affinity into closer focus, we may look at the groupings of meanings in Arabic which were, for Christian and Moslem Arabs and Arabic-speakers, parts of their common heritage. It bears a direct relationship to the sense of 'surrender' as the essence of religious practice: action to surrender, as distinct from ritual seen as an action, or from symbolism felt to be equal to action.

I am aware that there is a great deal of cultural and outward evidence for the elision of terms or the equating of concepts on a lower level during the Middle Ages. Take, for example, the direct evidence of alignment of thought shown by King Alfonso VIII of Leon and Castile (1158–1214) in his coinage. His *dinar* is still extant, with his title given in Arabic as Emir al-Qatuliqin ('Commander of the Catholics'), and the Pope's function defined as Imam al-Baya al-Masihiya

(Leader of the Community of the Messiah (Jesus), the Christian Church.* The mutual understanding is also very marked in Sicily.**

The existence of Sufi saints in Spain, where many Christian scholars of the Middle Ages studied, is witnessed both by copious documentation of their lives and also by books by, for instance, the Spaniard Ibn al-Arabi, one of the greatest Sufi masters. Professor Norman Cohn, among others, has written of the 'symbiosis' theory of Christian-Moslem experientialism, as well as giving a graphic resumé of some of the inter-changes between what are almost certainly the wilder elements among both parties:

> Towards the close of the 12th c. various Spanish cities, and notably Seville, witnessed the activities of mystical brotherhoods of Moslems. These people, who were known as Sufis, were 'holy beggars', who wandered in groups through the streets and squares, dressed in patched and parti-coloured robes. The novices among them were schooled in humiliation and self-abnegation: they had to dress in rags, to keep their eyes fixed on the ground, to eat revolting foodstuffs; and they owed blind obedi-ence to the master of the group. But once they

*Hitti, Professor Philip, *History of the Arabs*, New York (Macmillan) 1951 edition, p. 542.

**'Though himself an uncultured Christian, Roger I (died 1101) drew from the Moslems the mass of his infantry, patronised Arab learning, surrounded himself with Eastern philosophers, astrologers and physi-cians and allowed the non-Christians full liberty to follow their rites . . . Roger maintained the former system of administration and even kept high Moslem officials. His court at Palermo seemed more Oriental than Occidental. For over a century after this Sicily presented the unique spectacle of a Christian kingdom in which some of the highest positions were held by Moslems.' (Hitti, *History of the Arabs*, NY (Macmillan) 1951 ed., p. 607.

emerged from their noviciate, these Sufis entered a realm of total freedom. Disclaiming book-learning and theological subtleties, they rejoiced in direct knowledge of God—indeed, they felt themselves united with the divine essence in a most intimate union and this in turn liberated them from all restraints. Every impulse was experienced as a divine command; now they could surround themselves with wordly possessions, now they could live in luxury—and now, too, they could lie or steal or fornicate without qualms of conscience. For since inwardly the soul was wholly absorbed into God, external acts were of no account.

It is likely that Sufism, as it developed from the 9th c. onwards, itself owed much to certain mystical Christian sects in the East. In turn it seems to have assisted the growth of the mysticism of the Free Spirit in Christian Europe. Certainly every one of the features that characterized Sufism in 12th c. Spain—even to such details as particoloured robes —were to be noted as typical of the adepts of the Free Spirit a century or two later. In any case, around 1200 the cult of the Free Spirit began to emerge as an identifiable heresy in Western Christendom.*

Important though such correspondences undoubtedly are for historical purposes, and there are many of them, there is a deeper level of definition, the linguistic one, where the analysis of concepts brings a flavour of

*Cohn, N., *The Pursuit of the Millenium*, pp. 151f. I am indebted to Robert Cecil, Deputy-Chairman, School of European Studies, University of Reading, for this reference. The 'Free Spirit' heresy in Christianity is perhaps a good example of the application of some Sufic ideas and even practices without the necessary discipline.

the Moslem feeling for Islam and surrender and the possibility of the contemporary Christian understanding what this meant to the Moslem, so that he could compare it with his own conceptions.

It is, of course, widely known that the name of the religion of the Moslems is Islam, or Al-Islam, 'al' being the definite article in Arabic. Islam literally means 'submission, yielding, surrender'—to the will of God. 'Moslem' means one who is so surrendered. This etymology is important, because it is not just a name, it is a meaning. If you ask many an Arab, 'Are you a Moslem?' he will often reply, 'If God wills', which is roughly equivalent in colloquial speech to 'I hope so'. His attitude is that submission to the will of God is a matter of constant endeavour. Now we must also remember that there is a whole group of words derived from the radical SLM, which is the Arabic concept of 'surrender', any and all of which, almost, are associated with, regarded as inherently bound up with, each other and hence with Islam. By observing these words, we gain an idea as to the sense in which Islam has been understood by the people among whom it appeared, in their holy tongue, Arabic.

Surrender, then, is 'Islam', Associated with this is the word Salama(t), which means 'safety', 'security'. This fact is inextricably bound up in thinking with the direct relationship between submission to God and 'safety', that is, salvation. And Salama also stands for 'wholeness, soundness, faultlessness', to be made whole, safe, through submission. 'Heaven' is rendered by the term 'Dar as-Salam', the Abode of Peace, safety for man. To 'Salaam' a person is to wish him peace and wholeness. *Salim*, having been made whole, or sound, is another word from this root, like all the others an integral part of the vocabulary and daily speech of Arabic.*

Now that Islam is regarded as a means, a method, of arriving at peace and heaven is not in doubt either in the exegesis or in the occurrence of the word Sullam, again from the same root, which stands for an instrument or means, and including such things as a ladder or a stairway, and a tool, Finally, though this by no means exhausts our vocabulary of associated terms, there is Istilaam, which means receiving, and musaalim, one who is peaceful, lenient, clement.

It is impossible to exaggerate the significance of this constellation of terms and meanings: for the Arab-speaker they constitute the constant reminder of the diverse aspects of the religion and its meanings, and a permanent facility for confirming these concepts without having to rely only upon interpretation by later ideologists.

It has even been said by Moslem theoreticians that 'Islam is a word which denotes submission to the will of God; therefore it is not a noun like the name of a thing, but a conception which is the name of a thing as well.'

It is for this reason that, in the Quran, in the passage from Chapter 2, verse 103 which I quoted earlier, the sequence ends with the words which can be translated either as 'and to God we are resigned,' or 'we are Moslems'. Islam, as is well known, speaks of the true religious leaders, submitted to the will of God before the time of the Prophet Mohammed, as 'Moslems'. This is not only found in the Quran; I have heard my Afghan coreligionists say, often: 'Chi khub adam ast in

*Cf. discussion on these lines in Shah, Sirdar Ikbal Ali, *Lights of Asia*, London (Arthur Barker), 1934, pp. 6f.

58

Nasrani—Moslem ast'. This means, 'What a good man this Christian is—he is a Moslem'. Even though these words are in Persian and not in Arabic, the sense is preserved absolutely, having been transferred successfully to an Aryan language from a Semitic one, each having very little similarity one to the other.

The Quran itself cannot be translated, for this very reason: a part of the meaning will be rendered into the other language, but of course unless that language has (and this seems most unlikely) a constellation of concepts which exactly coincides with those of Arabic, the inbuilt pattern of concepts will inevitably be disturbed. I remember my own father using this very same illustration, employing the example of the radical SLM and its associations, to explain to me when I had just celebrated my eighth birthday in June, 1932. He was verifying passages from the rendition of the Quran by Mohammed Ali, and informing me why he was at that moment calling his selection '*from* the Quran'.*

*Shah, the Sirdar Ikbal Ali, *Extracts from the Koran*, London, (Blackie) 1933.

The affinity of Christian and Moslem mystics, basing their lives and practices on the conception of the surrender to God, has excited the interest of a very large number of thinkers.

I have already lectured on this subject at Sussex University:* and have published some of the references from Western authorities dealing with the question.** The product of deep research covering many years, dealing with the Islamic mystics' influence, sometimes claimed to be a determining one, in literature, terminology and practices, on such significant figures as the Blessed Ramon Lull, Roger Bacon, Dante, St. John of the Cross, St. Teresa of Avila, Duns Scotus, and many others, is a matter of record. Virtually all of this work has been done by Christian scholars: literary men, historians of religion, medievalists and orientalists.*** I have quoted, too, Western specialists who have noted even the ultimate elision of functions: the Moslem saint Haji Bektash identified with St. Charambolos**** of the Greeks, the Latin Brother Anselm of Turmeda found to be one and the same individual as the Sufi mystic Abdulla el-Tarjuman.*****

*Monograph; with references, reprinted as the Introduction to my *The Way of the Sufi*, London (Cape) 1968, 1971; and New York (Dutton) 1969, hardback; 1970, paperback; (in Italian: *La Strada del Sufi*, Roma (Ubaldini) 1971.
**_The Sufi_, London 1964, New York 1964; Paris 1972 (*Les Soufis*), and other editions.
***Cf. Shah, Idries: *The Sufis*, (Chap. V *et passim*) London (Allen) 1964; (Cape, paperback, 1969, 1971; Paris (*Les Soufis*), Payot, 1972; New York (Doubleday) 1964; (Doubleday Anchor paperback, 1971); original edition London 1966; second edition, 1968.
****Birge, Dr. J. K., *The Bektashi Order of Dervishes*, London, (Luzac) 1937, p. 39, N.3.
*****_Ibid._, xviii.

The late Abbot of Downside, author of *Western Mysticism** which is regarded as something of a classic, clearly states that 'placing himself definitely in the point of view of Catholic theology', God can give particular revelations and mystical gifts to Moslem mystics. He defines what is needed, from the Christian point of view, to make it possible for such events to come about:

'Only the enlightening motion, wholly interior, which should put his mind in perfect consonance with the supernatural revealed truth: the 'grace of faith' which God refuses to no sincere mind which is proposed the object of faith.**

In this he echoes the spirit of a passage about devotion in the Quran, which refers to worship becoming, as it were, a 'texture' of man's actions and thoughts:

'In the places of worship which God hath allowed
to be raised, that his name may therein be
remembered, so men praise him in the morning
and in the evening; men who neither merchandis-
ing nor traffic diverts from the remembrance of
God and the keeping up of prayer. . . .'***

And is there a stage, from the point of view of Christians, where understanding of surrender, in spirit and language, can come to pass? Certainly Father Cyprian Rice, the Dominican author, in a book which has the Nihil Obstat and Imprimatur of the Dominican

---

*Butler, Dom Cuthbert, *Western Mysticism*, London (Grey Arrow) 1960, p. 287.
**Ibid.
***Quran, 24: 36, 37.

and Diocesan authorities in Rome* looks forward to such an understanding:

'Whatever one's preconceptions or reservations' he says, 'it is difficult not to recognize a kinship between the Sufi spirit and vocabulary and those of the Christian saints and mystics.' He is certainly not looking for a derivative pattern, with Islamic ideas taken from Christianity, as so many other workers have tried to sustain. No evidence for this derivation has so far been adduced, and, indeed, Father Rice himself says: 'It is difficult to trace any scriptural or literary evidence of the propagation of Christian Teaching on Islamic mystical writers. . . .'**

That the experiences of the desert monks in the Middle East still provide a powerful context for the resumption of understanding based on a devotional spirit is shown by a recent monograph*** written by the eminent Coptic lay churchman Judge Hilmi Makram Ebeid. In his 'Possibilities of Eastern Moral Influence on Modern Civilisation' he reminds us of the original identity of interests of the Moslems and the Christian monks of the Egyptian deserts whose numbers, he says, may have at times exceeded half a million, of several nationalities. Their tradition lives on: the Christian community of Egypt today numbers about four million. Dr. Ebeid, in invoking the longstanding and powerful bonds between the Egyptian Christians and their Moslem fellow-countrymen, concludes with the general assertion that the revitalisation of spiritual

---

*Rice, Cyprian, O. O., *The Persian Sufis*, London, (Allen and Unwin) 1964.

**Ibid.*, p. 23.

***Research Monograph, 1972 (in: *Sufi Studies*, New York (Dutton) 1973.)

life in the modern world may well come through Islamic sources.

Father Rice, as a Catholic, echoes this feeling, where he looks forward to a special future role for Islamic spirituality as, he says: 'to make possible a welding of religious thought between East and West, a vital, ecumenical commingling and understanding, which will prove ultimately to be, in the truest sense, on both sides, a return to origins, to the original unity.'*

A man with a devout Protestant background, with parents who made their children Christians, was the late Professor A. J. Arberry, of Cambridge, who consecrated most of his working life to the investigation of Islamic devotional literature, more especially of Sufi mysticism. His feelings about the future of co-operation between East and West in the study and development of this subject are very plainly put in this passage:

'It is far from useless to look back into the pages of the distant past. Whether we are Muslims or not, we are all surely children of One Father; and it is therefore no impertinence, no irrelevancy, for the Christian scholar to aim at rediscovering those vital truths which made the Sufi movement so powerful an influence for good. If he may have the co-operation of his Muslim colleagues in this research—and the signs are not wanting that he will—together they may hope to unfold a truly remarkable and inspiring history of high human endeavour; together they may succeed in retracing a pattern of thought and behaviour which will supply the needs of many seeking the re-establishment of moral and spiritual values in these dark and threatening times.' Like Dr. Ebeid, Dr. Arberry leaves us in no doubt that the Sufi heritage may, in his belief, and in

*Cyprian Rice, *Op. cit.*, p. 10.

his words, 'meet the requirements of the modern and future man.'*

If some of these fervent and hopeful aspirations are thought over-enthusiastic, it can only be said that people will find in a subject that which corresponds to their own bias, at least initially. It seems possible that with the wide-ranging familiarisation with varieties of Christian and Moslem religious experience and writing that a balance of understanding may be struck. It is unfortunately true today, as during any time in the past, that individuals and coteries, basing their view upon narrow experience and perhaps even narrower (though concealed) prejudices, present their own religions, and those of others, with what amounts to distortion. The effects of this must be put down to psychology: some of it may even be a clinical responsibility.

Currently, in the East and West, there is so much publication and misinformation that only extensive reading will enable the student to form a useful opinion. Few Western readers, of course, reading many contemporary works on Islam and particularly in the mystical area, will be able to perceive, unless they have this sound grounding, that many of the writers, while genuflecting towards objectivity, are in fact ideologists: pursuing personal vendettas or biases, or trying to create a climate for the ultimate projection of a certain exclusive point of view, or—worse, though fortunately rarer—seeking personal prominence: precisely what Ghazzali warns against in his 'Abysmal Valley'.

Several Eastern propagandists, some of them occupying scholarly posts of one kind or another, use up much

*Arberry, A. J., *Sufism*, London (Allen & Unwin) 1963, 134f.

ink in attacking Western workers. There is certainly some ground for pointing out the unbalanced picture, created by personal bias in such figures as Nicholson*, whose attraction for Rumi and Sufism is in conflict with several forms of opposition, creating a bizarre dichotomy. As I say, this balance can be redressed without intensive personal attacks: by familiarity with the whole spectrum of the materials. Again, current vogues for what people are pleased to call 'mysticism', but what are in fact more easily explained as, in general, sociological phenomena cause a confusing situation for many. The occultist-minded and less-informed tend to read or absorb selectively, and choose agreeable (to them) passages even more selectively. They are victims of two things: (1) lack of a good grounding of information; and (2) the confusion by well-meant but maladroit literature.

In the second category come some quite hilarious developments. Surrender to God must mean a search for truth, and a corresponding diminution of egotism. Some of the present-day writers and speakers on this subject are so palpably motivated by egotism, and the process has gone so far, that the disciple of one man known as a spiritual teacher once shouted at me: 'I have been told by my teacher not to listen to anyone; and when he tells me to do something, I do it!' When

---

*E.g., his belief that the Sufis attack Islam (*Selected Poems from The Divani Shamsi Tabriz*, Cambridge (University Press) 1952 edition, xxvi; that 'it is not surprising that the Sufis should lack the psychological richness and variety which is found in Western mysticism' *The Idea of Personality in Sufism*, Lahore 1964, (reprint of Cambridge edition), p. 101; that Hujwiri 'was neither a profound mystic nor a precise thinker' (*The Kashf al-Mahjub*, London (Luzac) 1959 edition, p. xvii). He also states, in violation of all Sufi thought, that Sufis reached 'a purer religion and a higher morality than Islam could offer them.' (In *The Legacy of Islam*, 1968 edition, p. 238).

I explained to him that if he was not to listen to anyone he should not listen to his teacher, he was at first quite astonished. Because there had been so much talk of occultism and Sufism, I devoted a great deal of time, in *The Sufis*, to showing how occultist aspirations, based on transient greed for power and 'knowledge' were unworthy and ineffective and also, in many cases, stemmed only from the uncritical acceptance of a distorted tradition. It was, in the event, just as well that I did so. This has enabled me, for nearly ten years, to dissolve the aspirations of people who approach Islamic mysticism as if it were some sort of magical system which would give them power of enlightenment without training and discipline. It has been responsible for making it possible to shed those people who are in fact clinical cases and not primarily seekers after truth. But, as fast as one manages to establish this principle, fresh recruits, drawn from the readers of the real occultists—including people who think that they have a religious bias and will not investigate and describe the distortions which they are unconsciously provoking and perpetuating (while overtly opposing them), fresh recruits, brandishing these so-called 'serious' books, their hopes inflamed, clamour to be taught secrets.

This merry-go-round has reached such proportions that I have to deal with an average of 30 letters a day, many from the readers of the 'serious' books who have not had any opportunity of learning about the trivial misunderstood and vestigial nature of their metaphysics.

But while we are on this subject, it really must be stressed that this phenomenon is not new. Approximately a thousand years ago Ali al-Hujwiri in his *Kashf al-Mahjub* (Revelation of the Veiled), now recognised as a Sufi classic, emphasized that there were many mere imitators and people who practised what they imagined to be ecstatogenic processes without a suitable context.

Fortunately, by the process which is known these days as 'feedback'—measuring and assessing the results of what one does by people's reactions—it is possible to see these developments at work. Those who, failing to go a sufficient distance toward surrender to God, whether they be Christians or Moslems, can easily be shown, more especially in the light, too, of modern psychology, for what they are. This yields instructive study material with which we can demonstrate superficial and subjective states to honest enquirers; and there are indications that the initiators of such petty activities themselves can be reached by a similar method. There is a rag-bag of Eastern and Western individuals who specialise in making a good deal of noise in attempting to capture the attention of both Christians and Moslems for their peculiar brands of mystical study. Their efforts could only succeed to any extent at all if they themselves succeeded in confining students' attention to their own writings and activities. Any reasonable degree of familiarisation for the student with the whole range of available material (in the case of Sufis, with the major Sufi classics) which exist in translation, will at once show up the narrowness and selectivity of their pretensions. Even unreliable translations give enough material to fulfil this function.

The danger here, of course, is that the common human desire to seek a 'system', a limiting framework through which to work, an ideology which will apparently answer all questions, may tempt numbers of otherwise far more flexible, far-sighted and useful individuals to narrow their perspectives to one or more of the formulations which are offered by these would-be experts whose main distinguishing characteristic is often that in selecting one contention about mysticism they automatically ignore another, equally valid or emphatic, one, said, written or practised by our major teachers.

In the manifestation of the surrender to God as a way to salvation, therefore, the problem remains what it has always been: to avoid total generalisation as much as total narrowing of doctrine. This is not easy to learn and to practise, but it undoubtedly distinguishes the great teachers from the would-be ones; the one with interior perception of truth from those who imagine that they have it because they happen to 'specialise' in this or that, in other words, who have adopted an egotistical posture and seek to defend it by attacking other people and peddling a partial account of mystical information.

Thus, knowledge and understanding are vitally important prerequisites to the ability to surrender. A person does not 'surrender to God', in the sense in which this technical term is used by Christians and Moslems, merely by becoming a 'consumer of ideas or emotions'. There is a serious danger that the presentation of the 'surrender' concept may take on a titillating aspect where all that is stimulated is the *Amour propre*; where, above all, something which is a very definite procedure is mistaken for a somewhat easy 'golden key'. Modern psychology has done us the service of stating baldly that there must be a difference between modesty and maso-chism. And, as an example of how lack of information, or hinting in a certain manner, can arouse uncritical and even absurd expectations, I would like to give you an analogy from recent experience.

A little while ago, I began a talk in London with these words:

'There is a country where, for centuries, people have drunk, often first thing in the morning, a decoction of a certain dried herb, which they cause to be brought from distant and, to them, little-known lands. Many of them believe that they would not be able to manage their lives unless they consumed this nostrum regularly. They have fought wars over it, and in time of war they have taken immensely complicated and hazardous pains to ensure its continued supply. . . .'

At this point, someone stood up and said:

'What is this place, what is the herb? Can we get any, and would it be useful to us? Can we visit the country where it is used?'

There was a rustle of approval from the audience: this was what was in the minds of many, if not all, of them. I noticed that well over two-thirds of them seemed to be sitting on the edge of their seats.

Well, as I said at that time, yes, we can get the herb and it is useful to us, we are already in the country, and the plant is called 'tea'.

At that time, in Britain, this 'unknown' substance—tea—was being imported at the rate of 500 million lbs per annum. Every year, each man, woman and child in those islands (and in my audience) was already consuming, every year, the decoction of seven lbs of the stuff. . . .

One might say that such an experiment, which I and others have performed many times, is certain, when carried out among credulous, greedy, gullible people, to produce a reaction like this. I entirely agree; which brings me to the real point of the story. I have not yet told you who the audience were. The people at that lecture, who numbered over two hundred individuals, were all, so far as could be determined, people who had come to listen to a talk about the relationship of man with God, the possibility of self-improvement through faith, the bases of approaches to true humility. They had been selected from among groups of people who, for many years, had convinced themselves that they were seekers of truth, and certainly had had no hand in the shaping of the background of their thinking. They were an audience of people who believed that they were following the teachings, the writings and the traditions, of Christian mysticism. In the absence of some kind of 'feedback', they had apparently not reached the point where they had overcome or attenuated to any very visible degree, their very superficial greed, literally, for some kind of nostrum. If people who are not sympathetic towards the religious perspective were to replicate such an experiment, they would not use it as we do, as an admonition; they would—and many have—use it as a 'proof' that spirituality is a form of greed. The teaching, by both Christians and Moslems, over the centuries, that it is not enough to seek God, but that he must be sought in a certain way, and that if this is not understood it can be said to be worse than no search at all, since the 'search' can merely nurture greed, these teachings had, in respect to those people, gone by the board.

Some Sufi mystics in Islam have been fiercely criticised for allegedly forbidding their disciples to perform pilgrimages or carry out other holy activities until they were in a state in which they would not only benefit, but would not suffer through feeding the wrong part of themselves with a spurious experience. Yet, if you verify this sort of experiment for yourself— and there is no need to rely upon my statements, for your experimental material is everywhere—you will come to understand the thinking behind such strictures. Neither the teacher of religion nor the would-be practitioner dares, if he is in his right mind, to develop hypocrisy or abet its development by failing to observe the primary necessities, the prerequisites for an attempt at surrender to God.

BIBLIOGRAPHY

Ali, Syed Ameer, *A Short History of the Saracens*, London 1949.

Ali, Syed Nawab, *Some Moral and Religious Teachings of Al-Ghazzali*, Lahore 1960.

Arberry, Professor A. J., *Sufism*, London 1963.

Azzam Pasha, Abd al-Rahman, *The Eternal Message of Muhammad*, New York, 1965.

Birge, Dr. J. K., *The Bektashi Order of Dervishes*, London 1937.

Butler, G. C., *Kings and Camels*, New York 1960.

Butler, Dom Cuthbert, *Western Mysticism*, London 1960.

Denti Di Pirajno, Alberto, *A Cure for Serpents*, London 1965.

Guillaume, Professor A., *The Life of Muhammad*, London 1955.

„ (Co-Editor), *Legacy of Islam*, Oxford 1968.

Hitti, Professor Philip K., *History of the Arabs*, New York 1951.

International Year Book and Statesmen's Who's Who, London 1971.

Kritzeck, Professor James, *Anthology of Islamic Literature*, London 1964.

Middle East and North Africa, The (Europa), London 1969.

Nasr, Seyyid Hossein, *Ideals and Realities of Islam*, London 1971.

„ *Sufi Essays*, London 1972.

Nicholson, Professor R. A., (translator) *The Kashf al-Mahjub*, London 1959.

„ *The Idea of Personality in Sufism*, Lahore 1964.

„ *Selected Poems from the Divani Shamsi Tabriz*, Cambridge 1952.

Parrinder, Dr. G., *Jesus in the Qur'an*, London 1965.

Redhouse, James W., *Legends of the Sufis*, Kingston 1965.

Rice, C., *The Persian Sufis*, London 1964.

Saunders, John L., *The Muslim World on the Eve of Europe's Expansion*, New Jersey 1966.

Shah, Sirdar Ikbal Ali, *Coronation Book of Oriental Literature, The* (Preface by the Aga Khan), London 1937.

„ *Extracts from the Koran*, London 1933.

„ *Lights of Asia*, London 1934.

„ *Mohammed: The Prophet*, London 1932.

Sherwani, Haroon Khan, *Muslim Colonies in France, Northern Italy and Switzerland*, Lahore 1964.

Underhill, Evelyn, *The Mystic Way*, London 1913.

Watt, W. M., *The Faith and Practice of Al-Ghazzali*, London 1963.

World Muslim Gazeteer, Karachi 1964 (World Muslim Congress: *Motamar Al-Alam Al-Islami*).

Books by Idries Shah

Characteristics, Activity and Interaction of belief-systems

Oriental Magic, London 1956, 1969, 1970, 1973 (illustrated), Foreword by Professor Louis Marin.

Secret Lore of Magic, The, London 1957, many reprints up to 1971. (bibliographical study).

Sufis, The, London 1964, 1969, 1971. (Introduction by Robert Graves).

Tales of the Dervishes, London 1967, (3rd impression 1969), 1973.

Sufi Teachings and their Projection:

Book of the Book, The, London 1969 (3rd edition 1973).

Monastery, The Magic, London 1972.

Reflections, London 1968 (reprinted); enlarged edition 1969, rep. 1971.

Thinkers of the East, London 1971, 1972.

Way of the Sufi, The, London 1968, 1971, 1974.

Literature of Sufi relevance:

Dermis Probe, The, London 1970.

Dreams, Caravan of, London 1968, 1971, 1973.

Idiots, Wisdom of the, London 1969, second (enlarged) ed., 1971.

Beliefs and Practices:

Mecca, Destination, London 1957, third printing 1971.

Mulla Nasrudin Corpus:

Exploits of the Incomparable Mulla Nasrudin, The, London 1966, 4th impression 1969; 1973.

Pleasantries of the Incredible Mulla Nasrudin, The, London 1968, 1960.

Subtleties of the Inimitable Mulla Nasrudin, The, London 1973.

University Lectures:

Geneva University: *The Elephant in the Dark* (Christianity, Islam and the Sufis), London 1973.

Sussex University: *Sufi Ideas, Special Problems in the Study of,* London 1966, third edition 1974.

Recent publications of Relevance.

Abdullah, A., *et al., New Research on Current Philosophical Systems,* London 1968.

Davidson, R. W., (editor) *Documents on Contemporary Dervish Communities,* London 1966.

Foster, W., *Sufi Studies Today,* London 1968.

Index to Idries Shah's The Sufis, Kingston 1966.

Lewin, Professor L., (editor) *The Diffusion of Sufi Ideas in the West,* Boulder, 1972.

Ornstein, Professor R., *The Psychology of Consciousness,* Reading 1972 (Sufi and other systems in the light of modern investigation of brain-function).

Shabistari, Mahmud, *The Secret Garden* (Tr. Johnson Pasha) London 1969.

Williams, Professor L. F. Rushbrook (editor) *Sufi Studies East and West,* New York 1973. (Collected papers by 24 Orientalist and other scholars).

Documentation Collections:

(Considerations of Sufi thought in the East and West in recent years, mainly through the work of Idries Shah)

Reviews, Volume 1   Sixty articles, reviews and quotations from press, radio, television and reference works in Britain and abroad, London 1973.

Reviews, Volume 2   Seventy-five extracts, opinions of scholars, reviews, references, etc., from Britain and other countries. London 1973.

Reviews, Volume 3   Twenty-five Spanish-language articles, reviews, etc., on Sufi thought and its contemporary effect. London and Buenos Aires 1973.

Reviews, Volume 4   Persian, Arabic, Turkish, Urdu and Eastern and African considerations of Sufi activity and studies, with some English summaries. London and Damascus 1974.